III

alyssa baumgarten

BookLeaf Publishing

India | USA | UK

Presentation by *BookLeaf Publishing*

Web: www.bookleafpub.com

E-mail: info@bookleafpub.com

ISBN: 9789363311497

First edition 2024

to my friends—

the ones who first showed me,

"you're a poet"

thank you, thank you, thank you,

for believing.

ACKNOWLEDGEMENT

to my family—

I wouldn't be here to express my gratitude,
to write these words,
if not for you.

PREFACE

I learned of death when I was 3
reconvened in my twenties,
and I've been aware of myself
now I'm living as me
observing,
collecting memories, creating poetry,

to preface; the holy trinity
the father is
the son is
the holy spirit,
and this is my journey to "It"

my interpretation of a concept far beyond human
conscience.

I

can we speak the tongue of flowers?

with subliminal sonnets
of sweet serendipity?

it's the language only we know.

II

2

god is not a father
It is not strict or just
god is not a person
It bares no being
or bound by name

the more I learn what god is not,
the more I know the difference.

III

imagine a world
where a child asks you why their mother hung herself
in a room filled with hearts
now,
imagine the feeling
to watch a child ask the very same question
you once asked
when your father chose death over you,
and no one could answer your bleeding heart.

IV

2008.

"your mad or depressed
and you move on
but a person never really dies untill you forget them"

2024.

so forget-me-not
upon the baby blue flowers

the wish of a daughter—
I'll wonder
where you wander
there I pray for the day
should we meet one another.

V

I'm restless again, the usual night crawlers
this 4am sky paints a rosy pink color
the doppler of cars a familiar rhythm
oh happiest of birthdays, miss alyssum
I've never heard somebody laugh while dreaming
next to my sisters brings life a new meaning
the blinds cut my vision along with the shrink
a monopoly on misery with puppets on strings
swallow this pill pushed by white collar vices
hello!
and welcome,
to my quarter century crisis.

VI

eastbound I head, a landscape of nothingness
repeat the pattern I've etched upon the pedal
a long day of labor I'm predestined to wallow
most nights recall sorrow, yet this one I'm still
these hours of darkness now seem so inviting
lyrical notes mark this deafening loneliness
a meaningfully meaningless moment of silence
undoubtably a nightmare I've just awaken
for these heavenly bodies obscure my existence
I am nothing and everything all at once
this highway paves the road to freedom
a desolate path escorts me back home.

VII

what does dying feel like?

I imagine it's the same as lying on the carpet
thinking,
have I been here several days,
or several hours?
a blinking clock
enough pills to stop the thoughts
see the light,
but it's darkness
the moon abides by,
and watches
a stare down between pain
and peace from what haunts me.

VIII

I sat in the parking lot and cried after work.
I did it for years,
but this year was the worst
the hour drive,
a song would replay,
and I'm re-minded
I couldn't stop crying.
the tears never seemed to dry
an endless stream
not a dam to subside
moonlight,
quiet; it's time
strip myself bare,
no hearing ears,
no eyes in sight

suffocating my face in the sheets
choking sobs
that's grief, you can't breathe
alone,
is this stage 1 or stage 3?
the screaming,
reverberating along the ceiling

it was as if my body was leaking
every ounce of joy I had left in me.

IX

mind-fucked by mockery
I sort through the madness
young blood runs deeper
than my existential sadness

eagerly I listen
to the sounds of their chatter
spiraling down
I'm more mad than the hatter

blinded by misery
my demons take stage
a cat with nine lives
escapes from her cage

a jack of all trades
I'm known for this game
careful while crossing
the path of blue flames.

X

a picture speaks all the words we keep,
zoom in closely, I've met many with incongruities
who speak words unaware of their rhyme or the
reason
today they spoke commandments,
ten lines of hypocrisy one preaches to another
how sinners point the finger at sinners
shame appears different on thy brother
I was born from a bloodline of judgment

there is "love",
and there is unconditional loving.

XI

grief: it's like a mute button.

imagine your own existence
a cinematic transcription
each encounter unscripted
unaware of the glare
off the window to one unseen—
and one mutes the screen.

now you are your own viewer,
to a life you remember
when you knew nothing
subtitles precede,
now things are things?
you don't know now
why anything means what it means
you conscientiously attempt
forgo the mind float adrift
now knowing, yet unknowing
that any moment
we are subject to nothingness
what once were your legs running in the grass
playing,
become anxious conversations evading
the cruelties of nature
they become characters,
and you're not there
you're just watching.

XII

today it brought forth patience,

when she smiled,
"look, see the wild berries"
red, ripe, garnet droplets
fingers stained in scarlet
I warned her, thorns!
one, two, leaves of..

—wait.
of III.
poison ivy?

I knew it.

there is a momentary breath
between real and false narratives.

XIII

gut feeling, I feel it
a drop off,
there's a difference
it's been long since I've had premonition
bubbling,
my blood is simmering
 a shower to wash the thoughts away
it's not working
what the fuck is happening?
shaking,
don'tscream don'tscream don'tscream,

breatheeeee, It tells me
 3 breaths in....in & out, again.

spiraling, spiraling, spiraling
a levy broken
waterworks,
I let the current run
the shoreline — it's gone.
no longer safe,
no more sound.
heaving,
do not fight, remain calm.

cotton robe soaked
muffled misery

dreading, a never ending loop

I mind myself — a story
a hypothetical does not mean a theory.

XIV

if I bite my tongue,
the words fade crimson rusted
ferrous drips of blood
my thoughts recoil back,
do I share my opinion?
my two cents?
stir in silence?
pull the trigger?
a response becomes a self-inflicted loaded gun,
regardless
so It told me,
Alyssa
there is no right, no wrong
you decide what you want
whether spoken or act upon
your behavior is chosen
you choose the consequence upon action
the reaction?
a lesson to learn from.

XV

more
moremoremore
how much more
until the next bout of boredom
the next wave
the next some-thing
you will learn it means no-thing.
really,
I've frequent Paris
I've grazed London
I've skipped along wildflowers
all summer long up in Scotland
floating off the coast of Dubrovnik
skipping stones atop snow capped mountains
watching ripples
where fjords reflect crystal clear waters
midnight soup in Herzegovina
I've sat 'round a table
of my people east in Poland
white & green down in Mexico,

and I've learned most are hopeless
most are coping by numbing
some so desperate
for dreams they thought they always dreamed of
for feeling,
for any-thing to make them see life as worth living,

so I've learned to live life for myself
a life free of expectations
a life I have accepted
no strings attached,
in a world where attachment is the root of all
suffering

& wisdom is giving
less is more, you cannot keep things.

XVI

I did not know
that I was the source of my own suffering
I did not know
I was the solution I was seeking

I spent, what?
16 years inquiring myself the same question
how do I be happy?

until I found the answer today,
and decided that I wanted to.

XVII

the card: what is something I need to let go?
...

the regret of missed moments
before the last of us unknown
it haunts you
on a spring afternoon,
when the flowers are in bloom
you replay those days long ago

casting shadows
rays a light
my silhouette aglow
hand in hand that darkness,
never fades, no, grieving is lifelong.

so he tells me
"the guilt, you need to let it go."

XVIII

shhhhh…

begin by listening.
the outside noises,
observe the distraction
those thoughts— remove them
every wave is connected
find your frequency, try to tune in

wake the senses
breathe in
breathe out,
oxygen
a force that gives and takes with it
the difference between life & death

take a moment
appreciate our place in the universe.

XIX

death is letting go
it's letting go of the physical form
the vehicle you have used to experience this
exhibition we call "life"
who we are is not the career
the currency we possess
the role we attempt to play in society,
to relieve the anxiety of being "something"

once I realized nothing has inherently any meaning,
not in a nihilistic sense,
but we ourselves have created the meaning
of the things we question the meaning of

that's when I met death
I learned only I know I exist,
this world was not designed to make sense

at the end of "this" life as you know yourself,
Alyssa,
a meaning someone gave upon birth
the soul rips—
physicality is finally stripped

you're free.

from all labels, objects, and objectives,
the words you have used to create an identity with
you become something greater than yourself.

XX

do not fear death!
trust me,
heaven is my favorite fantasy
how excruciating can nothingness be?

XXI.

The Mirror.
look upon me
who do you see?
the child who inquired
her dead father,
or me?
fates intertwined
time-lapsed back in time
bordering the line
between real and sublime
I was alive above my body
gazing beneath
the blind man's string
cat's cradled you to me
as if,
I may drift beyond the infinite
if not for the night you held my hand
and whispered softly,
I believe.
///

The Harrowing of Hell.
descend beside me
the gates reveal themselves
if I have not already
crucified myself,
could sainthood be way of
this messianic mania?

does the fragrance of divinity
mask the scent of my insanity?
god grant me serenity
interlude the persecutory
did I not warn?
of the seas of disorder?
I oscillate in waves
one pole to the other
to and fro
where did my eyes go?
I do not know how to feel
which thought is real?
if my words ring honest
am I patient or prophet?
and when I spoke to his spirit—
I was diseased.
time turns to violence
when you suffer in silence
the curse of my own father
sealing fate upon daughter
I know how I will die;

secretly.

The Dreamriver.
close your eyes
I remember us
high above in my dreams
meadows of memories
I have never received
when lilacs last
in the dooryard bloom'd

waltzing in unity
and for a brief moment, we were—
this feeling,
past, present and future
tried and true
our soul split in two
my reflection of me
mirrored prisms of you

The Last Beginning.
peer through the window
seven rays for each sorrow
heaven knows!
behind every decision,
whether harmony or dissonance
is God not a reason
for us to find meaning?
that knowing feeling
of quiet intuition
this—
the eternal provision

The Golden Era.
an ever-returning spring
I raise a flower in prayer
sowing the seeds I once grieved
angels surrounding
and just when I sing;
the hymns of solitude
halcyon blue
hues of déjà vu

a thought unsaid
I meet myself, again.

III.